EMPOWERING E-COMMERCE:
HARNESSING AI FOR SHOPIFY DESIGN

BY
HENRY E. PARKINS

COPYRIGHT PAGE

Right reserved, no part of the

Publication may be republished

In any form or by any means,

Including photo copy, scanning

Or otherwise without prior written

Permission to the copyright

Holder Copyright @2024

HENRY E. PARKINS

TABLE OF CONTENTS

INTRODUCTION

In the dynamic landscape of modern commerce, the digital realm stands as a beacon of opportunity and innovation. E-commerce, the process of buying and selling goods and services online, has revolutionized the way businesses connect with consumers, transcending geographical boundaries and temporal constraints. At the heart of this revolution lies platforms like Shopify, offering entrepreneurs and established brands alike the tools to create, manage, and scale their online stores with unprecedented ease and efficiency.

"E empowering E-Commerce: Harnessing AI for Shopify Design" delves into the intersection of technology and commerce, exploring how artificial intelligence (AI) can transform the design landscape of Shopify stores to enhance user experiences, drive conversions, and propel business growth. As businesses strive to differentiate themselves in an increasingly competitive market, harnessing the power of AI becomes not just a choice but a strategic imperative.

Before we plunge into the depths of AI-driven Shopify design, it's essential to understand the foundational pillars of e-commerce and the pivotal role Shopify plays in shaping online retail ecosystems.

E-Commerce: Redefining Commerce in the Digital Age

The advent of e-commerce represents a paradigm shift in the way transactions occur, challenging traditional brick-and-mortar models and fostering a new era of consumer engagement. With the click of a button, shoppers can explore a vast array of products, compare prices, read reviews, and make purchases from the comfort of their homes or on the go.

The allure of e-commerce lies not only in its convenience but also in its ability to democratize entrepreneurship, empowering individuals and businesses of all sizes to enter the global marketplace with minimal barriers to entry. From artisanal crafts to multinational corporations, e-commerce offers a level playing field where innovation and creativity reign supreme.

Yet, amidst the boundless opportunities of the digital marketplace, businesses face the daunting task of standing out amidst the digital noise, capturing the attention of discerning consumers, and fostering lasting relationships built on trust and value.

Enter Shopify: Empowering Entrepreneurs, Fueling Innovation

In the bustling ecosystem of e-commerce platforms, Shopify emerges as a trailblazer, offering a comprehensive suite of tools and services tailored to the needs of online merchants. Founded on the principles of simplicity, flexibility, and scalability, Shopify empowers entrepreneurs to bring their visions to life, from fledgling startups to thriving enterprises.

At its core, Shopify serves as more than just a platform; it's a catalyst for innovation, a gateway to digital entrepreneurship, and a hub for creativity and commerce to converge. With its intuitive interface, robust features, and extensive app ecosystem, Shopify enables merchants to design captivating storefronts, streamline operations, and unlock new avenues for growth.

As the digital landscape evolves and consumer expectations soar, the role of design in shaping the e-commerce experience becomes increasingly paramount. From the layout of a homepage to the seamless navigation of product pages, design serves as the cornerstone of a compelling and cohesive brand narrative, drawing customers in and guiding them on a journey of discovery and delight.

In the pages that follow, we embark on a transformative journey into the realm of AI-driven Shopify design, exploring the myriad ways in which artificial intelligence can revolutionize the e-commerce landscape, elevate the Shopify experience, and empower merchants to thrive in an ever-changing digital landscape. Through real-world examples, practical insights, and forward-thinking strategies, we illuminate the path towards e-commerce excellence, where innovation knows no bounds, and possibilities abound.

CHAPTER 1

DEFINITION AND IMPORTANCE OF E-COMMERCE

E-commerce, short for electronic commerce, is the process of buying and selling goods and services over the internet. It encompasses a broad spectrum of transactions, ranging from online retail stores and digital marketplaces to business-to-business (B2B) exchanges and online auctions. At its core, e-commerce transcends traditional physical boundaries, enabling businesses and consumers to engage in commerce anytime, anywhere, with unparalleled convenience and accessibility.

In the digital age, e-commerce has emerged as a cornerstone of modern commerce, reshaping the way goods and services are bought, sold, and consumed. It leverages digital technologies to streamline transactions, eliminate geographic constraints, and facilitate seamless interactions between buyers and sellers across the globe. Whether it's purchasing a pair of shoes from an online retailer, booking a hotel room through a travel website, or subscribing to a streaming service for entertainment, e-commerce has permeated nearly every aspect of our daily lives.

The importance of e-commerce extends far beyond its convenience and accessibility. It serves as a catalyst for economic growth, driving innovation, fostering entrepreneurship, and expanding market opportunities for businesses of all sizes. By lowering the barriers to entry and democratizing access to global markets, e-commerce empowers individuals and businesses to reach new audiences, forge meaningful connections, and build sustainable revenue streams.

Furthermore, e-commerce offers unparalleled insights into consumer behavior, preferences, and trends, enabling businesses to harness the power of data-driven decision-making and tailor their offerings to meet evolving customer needs. Through advanced analytics, businesses can optimize marketing campaigns, personalize user experiences, and enhance customer engagement, fostering long-term loyalty and brand advocacy.

In today's hyper-connected world, where digital transformation is reshaping industries and redefining customer expectations, embracing e-commerce is not just a competitive advantage—it's a strategic imperative. Businesses that fail to adapt to the shifting tides of digital commerce risk being left behind, relegated to the sidelines as more agile competitors seize the reins of innovation and chart a course towards sustainable growth and success.

As we embark on a journey to explore the convergence of e-commerce and artificial intelligence (AI) within the Shopify ecosystem, it's crucial to recognize the pivotal role that e-commerce plays in shaping the future of commerce. By harnessing the transformative power of technology, we have the opportunity to unlock new frontiers of possibility, reimagine the e-commerce experience, and empower businesses to thrive in a rapidly evolving digital landscape.

In the pages that follow, we delve deeper into the intersection of e-commerce and AI, exploring how innovative technologies and forward-thinking strategies can revolutionize the Shopify design landscape, elevate user experiences, and propel businesses towards e-commerce excellence. Join us as we embark on a journey of discovery, innovation, and empowerment where the possibilities are limitless, and the future of e-commerce is ours to shape.

Overview of Shopify as an E-Commerce Platform

In the bustling landscape of e-commerce platforms, Shopify stands as a beacon of innovation, empowerment, and entrepreneurship. Since its inception in 2006, Shopify has evolved from a simple e-commerce solution into a comprehensive platform that powers millions of online stores across the globe. At its core, Shopify empowers merchants to bring their visions to life, streamline operations, and scale their businesses with unparalleled ease and efficiency.

Central to Shopify's appeal is its user-friendly interface, which caters to both novice entrepreneurs and seasoned professionals alike. With its intuitive drag-and-drop editor, customizable themes, and built-in tools, Shopify enables merchants to design captivating storefronts that reflect their brand identity and resonate with their target audience. From sleek and minimalist designs to bold and immersive experiences, Shopify offers a myriad of options to suit every aesthetic preference and business requirement.

Moreover, Shopify boasts a robust ecosystem of apps, plugins, and integrations, allowing merchants to extend the platform's functionality and tailor their stores to meet specific needs. Whether it's adding social media integration, implementing advanced analytics, or integrating with third-party payment gateways, Shopify's App Store offers a treasure trove of solutions to enhance the e-commerce experience and drive business growth.

Beyond its design and functionality, Shopify excels in its ability to simplify the complexities of online commerce, from inventory management and order processing to shipping and fulfillment. With built-in features like inventory tracking, automatic tax calculation, and shipping rate calculators, Shopify streamlines the operational aspects of running an online store, freeing merchants to focus on what they do best building relationships with customers and driving sales.

Furthermore, Shopify's dedication to security, reliability, and scalability sets it apart as a trusted partner for businesses of all sizes. With enterprise-grade infrastructure, 24/7 customer support, and industry-leading security protocols, Shopify provides merchants with the peace of mind they need to navigate the ever-changing landscape of e-commerce with confidence and assurance.

In recent years, Shopify has emerged as more than just a platform for online sales it's a catalyst for innovation, a community of like-minded entrepreneurs, and a driving force behind the democratization of commerce. Through initiatives like Shopify Partners and Shopify Plus, the platform empowers developers, agencies, and high-growth enterprises to push the boundaries of what's possible, innovate at scale, and unlock new opportunities for success.

As we embark on a journey to explore the intersection of Shopify and artificial intelligence (AI) within the realm of e-commerce design, it's clear that Shopify's commitment to innovation and empowerment knows no bounds. By harnessing the power of AI-driven insights, automation, and personalization, Shopify enables merchants to create immersive, data-driven experiences that captivate audiences, drive conversions, and fuel long-term growth.

In the pages that follow, we delve deeper into the transformative potential of AI in Shopify design, exploring how innovative technologies and forward-thinking strategies can revolutionize the e-commerce landscape and empower merchants to thrive in an increasingly competitive marketplace. Join us as we unlock the secrets to e-commerce success, where Shopify serves as the canvas, and AI as the brush, painting a future of boundless possibility and untapped potential.

Significance of Design in E-Commerce Success

In the digital age, where attention spans are fleeting and competition is fierce, the significance of design in e-commerce success cannot be overstated. Beyond mere aesthetics, design serves as the cornerstone of a compelling and cohesive brand narrative, shaping perceptions, influencing behaviors, and driving meaningful connections with consumers. As the gateway to the online shopping experience, design plays a pivotal role in capturing attention, fostering engagement, and ultimately, converting visitors into loyal customers.

First Impressions Matter: In the crowded landscape of e-commerce, first impressions are often the only chance to make a lasting impact. A well-designed storefront not only captivates attention but also instills trust and credibility in the minds of consumers. From visually stunning imagery to intuitive navigation, every aspect of design contributes to shaping the initial perception of a brand and its offerings.

User Experience is Key: At the heart of effective e-commerce design lies user experience (UX) the art of crafting seamless and intuitive interactions that delight and inspire. A user-centric approach to design ensures that visitors can effortlessly navigate the site, find what they're looking for, and complete transactions with ease. From streamlined checkout processes to mobile-responsive layouts, prioritizing UX design fosters customer satisfaction and loyalty, driving repeat business and word-of-mouth referrals.

Brand Identity and Differentiation: In a sea of online competitors, brand identity serves as a beacon of distinction, setting businesses apart from the crowd and forging emotional connections with consumers. Through thoughtful design elements such as logos, color palettes, typography, and imagery, brands can convey their unique personality, values, and story, resonating with target audiences on a deeper level. By leveraging design to cultivate a memorable and cohesive brand identity, businesses can carve out a distinct niche in the marketplace and foster long-term relationships with customers.

Visual Merchandising and Product Presentation:

In the absence of physical storefronts, visual merchandising takes center stage in the e-commerce landscape, guiding shoppers on a virtual journey of discovery and delight. Strategic product placement, compelling imagery, and immersive storytelling transform mundane transactions into memorable experiences, enticing customers to explore, engage, and ultimately, make purchase decisions. By leveraging design principles to showcase products in their best light, businesses can increase conversion rates, boost average order values, and drive bottom-line results.

Optimization for Conversion and Performance:

Beyond aesthetics, effective e-commerce design encompasses a holistic approach to optimization, balancing creativity with data-driven insights to maximize conversion rates and performance metrics. Through A/B testing, heat mapping, and user behavior analysis, businesses can identify pain points, uncover hidden opportunities, and fine-tune their design strategies to align with customer preferences and business objectives. By iterating and optimizing design elements over time, businesses can stay agile, responsive, and poised for sustained growth in a rapidly evolving marketplace.

As we navigate the intricacies of e-commerce design within the Shopify ecosystem, it's imperative to recognize the transformative power of design in shaping the online shopping experience. By prioritizing design excellence, businesses can create immersive, memorable, and meaningful interactions that inspire loyalty, drive sales, and elevate the e-commerce journey to new heights of success. In the pages that follow, we explore how artificial intelligence (AI) can amplify the impact of design, revolutionizing the way businesses engage with customers, optimize user experiences, and unlock the full potential of their Shopify stores. Join us as we embark on a journey of innovation, empowerment, and e-commerce excellence, where design serves as the catalyst for transformation and the key to unlocking limitless possibilities.

EMPOWERING E-COMMERCE: HARNESSING AI FOR SHOPIFY DESIGN

CHAPTER 2

UNDERSTANDING AI IN E-COMMERCE

Artificial Intelligence (AI) stands at the forefront of technological innovation, reshaping industries, redefining consumer experiences, and revolutionizing the way businesses operate in the digital age. In the realm of e-commerce, AI holds immense potential to transform every facet of the online shopping journey, from discovery and engagement to conversion and retention. By harnessing the power of machine learning, data analytics, and predictive algorithms, AI empowers businesses to unlock actionable insights, automate tedious tasks, and deliver personalized experiences at scale.

Definition and Scope of AI: At its core, AI refers to the simulation of human intelligence in machines, enabling them to perform tasks that typically require human cognition, such as learning, reasoning, and problem-solving. In the context of e-commerce, AI encompasses a broad spectrum of technologies and applications, including natural language processing (NLP), computer vision, recommendation engines, chatbots, and predictive analytics. By leveraging vast amounts of data and sophisticated algorithms, AI enables businesses to derive valuable insights, anticipate customer needs, and optimize decision-making processes in real-time.

Role of AI in E-Commerce: In the dynamic landscape of online commerce, AI serves as a catalyst for innovation, empowering businesses to stay ahead of the curve, adapt to evolving consumer preferences, and capitalize on emerging trends. From personalized product recommendations to dynamic pricing strategies, AI enables businesses to enhance customer engagement, drive conversions, and foster long-term loyalty. Moreover, AI-powered analytics provide businesses with deeper visibility into customer behavior, market trends, and competitive landscapes, enabling them to make informed decisions and seize opportunities for growth.

Benefits of AI in E-Commerce: The benefits of AI in e-commerce are manifold, spanning every stage of the customer journey and beyond. By analyzing vast datasets in real-time, AI can identify patterns, detect anomalies, and uncover hidden insights that traditional analytics tools may overlook. Through predictive analytics, businesses can anticipate customer preferences, forecast demand, and optimize inventory management, reducing costs and minimizing risks. Furthermore, AI-powered chatbots and virtual assistants provide personalized support and assistance to customers, enhancing the overall shopping experience and driving satisfaction.

Enhancing Personalization and User Experience: One of the most compelling aspects of AI in e-commerce is its ability to deliver hyper-personalized experiences tailored to individual preferences and behaviors. By analyzing historical data, browsing patterns, and purchase history, AI can create personalized product recommendations, curated content, and targeted promotions that resonate with each customer on a deeper level. Through dynamic pricing algorithms and personalized offers,

businesses can incentivize purchases, increase average order values, and foster repeat business, driving revenue and profitability.

Challenges and Considerations:

While the potential of AI in e-commerce is vast, it's essential for businesses to navigate potential challenges and ethical considerations associated with its implementation. Concerns related to data privacy, algorithmic bias, and transparency require careful consideration and proactive measures to mitigate risks and uphold consumer trust. Moreover, the complexity and cost of implementing AI solutions may pose barriers for smaller businesses, necessitating thoughtful planning and strategic investment to maximize ROI.

As we embark on a journey to explore the intersection of AI and Shopify design, it's clear that AI holds the key to unlocking new frontiers of possibility and empowering businesses to thrive in an increasingly competitive marketplace. By harnessing the transformative power of AI, businesses can elevate the e-commerce experience, drive meaningful engagement, and unlock the full potential of their Shopify stores. In the pages that follow, we delve deeper into the practical applications of AI in Shopify design, exploring how innovative technologies and forward-thinking strategies can revolutionize the way businesses connect with customers, optimize user experiences, and achieve e-commerce excellence. Join us as we unlock the secrets to success in the AI-driven era of e-commerce, where the possibilities are limitless, and the future is ours to shape.

Definition and Concept of Artificial Intelligence

Artificial Intelligence (AI) represents the pinnacle of technological innovation, encompassing a diverse array of disciplines, methodologies, and applications aimed at replicating human intelligence in machines. At its core, AI seeks to imbue machines with the ability to perceive, reason, learn, and adapt in ways that mimic or even surpass the capabilities of the human mind.

In the context of e-commerce and Shopify design, AI serves as a transformative force, empowering businesses to unlock new dimensions of creativity, efficiency, and customer engagement. At its essence, AI enables machines to analyze vast datasets, detect patterns, and make data-driven decisions in real-time, revolutionizing every aspect of the online shopping experience.

The concept of AI encompasses a spectrum of technologies and techniques, each designed to tackle specific challenges and achieve distinct objectives within the e-commerce ecosystem. From machine learning and natural language processing to computer vision and predictive analytics, AI enables businesses to harness the power of data to drive innovation, optimize processes, and deliver personalized experiences at scale.

At its foundation, AI operates on the principles of automation, optimization, and adaptation, leveraging algorithms and models to automate repetitive tasks, optimize resource allocation, and adapt to changing environments and user preferences. Through continuous learning and iteration, AI algorithms refine their understanding of complex data patterns, uncover actionable insights, and evolve in response to emerging trends and challenges.

In the context of e-commerce design, AI enables businesses to create immersive, data-driven experiences that resonate with customers, drive conversions, and foster long-term loyalty. From personalized product recommendations and dynamic pricing strategies to AI-powered chatbots and virtual assistants, AI enhances every touchpoint of the customer journey, elevating the e-commerce experience to new heights of sophistication and engagement.

As we explore the intersection of AI and Shopify design, it's important to recognize the transformative potential of AI as a catalyst for innovation, empowerment, and growth. By harnessing the power of AI-driven insights, automation, and personalization, businesses can unlock new opportunities for creativity, differentiation, and success in an increasingly competitive marketplace. In the pages that follow, we delve deeper into the practical applications of AI in Shopify design, exploring how innovative technologies and forward-thinking strategies can revolutionize the way businesses connect with customers, optimize user experiences, and achieve e-commerce excellence. Join us as we embark on a journey of discovery, innovation, and empowerment, where the possibilities are limitless, and the future is ours to shape.

The Role of AI in E-Commerce:

Artificial Intelligence (AI) stands as a transformative force in the realm of e-commerce, reshaping the landscape of online retail and revolutionizing the way businesses interact with customers, optimize operations, and drive growth. At its core, AI empowers businesses to leverage data-driven insights, automate tedious tasks, and deliver personalized experiences at scale, unlocking new dimensions of creativity, efficiency, and innovation in the e-commerce ecosystem.

Personalization and Customer Engagement:

One of the most compelling aspects of AI in e-commerce is its ability to deliver hyper-personalized experiences tailored to individual preferences and behaviors. By analyzing vast datasets encompassing customer interactions, browsing history, purchase patterns, and demographic information, AI algorithms can generate personalized product recommendations, curated content, and targeted promotions that resonate with each customer on a deeper level. Through dynamic pricing algorithms, businesses can optimize pricing strategies in real-time, adapting to market conditions and customer dynamics to maximize conversion rates and drive revenue.

Predictive Analytics and Demand Forecasting: AI-powered predictive analytics enables businesses to anticipate customer needs, forecast demand, and optimize inventory management with unprecedented accuracy and precision. By analyzing historical data, market trends, and external factors, AI algorithms can predict future demand patterns, identify emerging trends, and optimize inventory levels to prevent stockouts and overstocking. Moreover, AI-driven demand forecasting enables businesses to optimize supply chain

operations, reduce carrying costs, and minimize the risk of excess inventory, enhancing operational efficiency and profitability.

Enhanced Customer Service and Support:

AI-powered chatbots and virtual assistants provide businesses with a scalable and cost-effective solution to deliver personalized customer service and support across multiple channels. By leveraging natural language processing (NLP) and machine learning algorithms, chatbots can engage customers in real-time conversations, answer inquiries, provide product recommendations, and facilitate transactions seamlessly. Furthermore, AI-driven sentiment analysis enables businesses to gauge customer satisfaction levels, identify potential issues, and proactively address concerns, fostering trust and loyalty among customers.

Fraud Detection and Security:

In the dynamic landscape of e-commerce, fraud detection and security remain paramount concerns for businesses and consumers alike. AI-powered fraud detection systems leverage advanced machine learning algorithms to analyze transaction data, detect anomalous patterns, and identify potential instances of fraudulent activity in real-time. By monitoring transactional behavior, IP addresses, device fingerprints, and other contextual signals, AI algorithms can distinguish legitimate transactions from fraudulent ones, mitigating financial losses and protecting sensitive customer information.

Dynamic Pricing and Revenue Optimization:

AI-driven dynamic pricing algorithms enable businesses to optimize pricing strategies based on real-time market conditions, competitor pricing, and customer dynamics. By analyzing historical data, demand elasticity, and competitive positioning, AI algorithms can adjust prices dynamically to maximize revenue, increase profit margins, and capitalize on opportunities for growth. Moreover, AI-powered pricing optimization enables businesses to implement personalized pricing strategies, loyalty incentives, and promotional offers that resonate with individual customers, driving customer engagement and loyalty over time.

In summary, the role of AI in e-commerce extends far beyond automation and optimization it serves as a catalyst for innovation, empowerment, and growth. By harnessing the power of AI-driven insights, automation, and personalization, businesses can unlock new opportunities for creativity, differentiation, and success in an increasingly competitive marketplace. In the pages that follow, we delve deeper into the practical applications of AI in Shopify design, exploring how innovative technologies and forward-thinking strategies can revolutionize the way businesses connect with customers, optimize user experiences, and achieve e-commerce excellence. Join us as we embark on a journey of discovery, innovation, and empowerment, where the possibilities are limitless, and the future is ours to shape.

Benefits of Integrating AI into Shopify Design

The integration of Artificial Intelligence (AI) into Shopify design heralds a new era of innovation, empowerment, and growth in the realm of e-commerce. By harnessing the power of AI-driven insights, automation, and personalization, businesses can unlock new opportunities to optimize user experiences, drive conversions, and foster long-term customer loyalty. In the pages that follow, we explore the myriad benefits of integrating AI into Shopify design and the transformative impact it can have on the e-commerce landscape.

Personalized User Experiences:

AI enables businesses to deliver hyper-personalized experiences tailored to the unique preferences and behaviors of individual customers. By analyzing vast datasets encompassing customer interactions, browsing history, and purchase patterns, AI algorithms can generate personalized product recommendations, curated content, and targeted promotions that resonate with each customer on a deeper level. Through AI-driven personalization, businesses can enhance engagement, increase conversion rates, and foster lasting relationships with customers.

Dynamic Content Optimization:

AI-powered content optimization enables businesses to create dynamic and engaging experiences that adapt in real-time based on user interactions and behaviors. Through A/B testing, multivariate testing, and predictive analytics, AI algorithms can optimize content elements such as images, headlines, and calls-to-action to maximize engagement and drive conversions. By continuously refining content strategies based on data-driven insights, businesses can increase visibility, improve click-through rates, and enhance the overall effectiveness of their Shopify stores.

Automated Design Optimization:

AI streamlines the process of design optimization by automating repetitive tasks, identifying areas for improvement, and implementing changes dynamically based on performance metrics. Through machine learning algorithms, AI can analyze user interactions, heatmaps, and conversion funnels to identify friction points and opportunities for enhancement within Shopify designs. By automating design optimization processes, businesses can iterate rapidly, uncover insights, and iterate on design elements to create more compelling and effective user experiences.

Enhanced Product Discovery and Recommendations: AI-powered product discovery and recommendation engines enable businesses to guide users on a personalized journey of exploration and discovery. By analyzing user behavior, purchase history, and contextual signals, AI algorithms can surface relevant products, accessories, and complementary items that align with each customer's preferences and interests. Through AI-driven recommendations, businesses can increase average order values, reduce bounce rates, and inspire users to explore additional offerings within their Shopify stores.

Predictive Analytics for Sales and Inventory Management: AI-driven predictive analytics empower businesses to anticipate demand, optimize inventory levels, and mitigate stockouts and overstocking. By analyzing historical sales data, market trends, and external factors, AI algorithms can forecast future demand patterns, identify seasonal trends, and optimize inventory allocation across product categories and locations. Through predictive analytics, businesses can reduce carrying costs, minimize the risk of stockouts, and optimize supply chain operations to ensure seamless fulfillment and customer satisfaction.

Efficient Customer Support and Engagement: AI-powered chatbots and virtual assistants provide businesses with scalable and cost-effective solutions to deliver personalized customer support and engagement across multiple channels. By leveraging natural language processing (NLP) and machine learning algorithms, chatbots can engage customers in real-time conversations, answer inquiries, resolve issues, and facilitate transactions seamlessly. Through AI-driven customer support, businesses can improve response times, enhance satisfaction levels, and reduce the burden on human support agents.

In summary, the integration of AI into Shopify design offers a multitude of benefits that empower businesses to create more compelling, personalized, and effective user experiences. By leveraging AI-driven insights, automation, and personalization, businesses can optimize user engagement, drive conversions, and foster long-term customer loyalty in an increasingly competitive e-commerce landscape. In the pages that follow, we delve deeper into the practical applications of AI in Shopify design, exploring how innovative technologies and forward-thinking strategies can revolutionize the way businesses connect with customers and achieve e-commerce excellence. Join us as we embark on a journey of discovery, innovation, and empowerment, where the possibilities are limitless, and the future is ours to shape.

CHAPTER 3

LEVERAGING AI FOR SHOPIFY DESIGN

In the dynamic world of e-commerce, where innovation and customer experience reign supreme, the integration of Artificial Intelligence (AI) into Shopify design represents a paradigm shift in how businesses engage with customers, optimize user experiences, and drive growth. By harnessing the power of AI-driven insights, automation, and personalization, businesses can unlock new dimensions of creativity, efficiency, and effectiveness in designing compelling and immersive storefronts on the Shopify platform. In the pages that follow, we explore the myriad ways in which businesses can leverage AI for Shopify design to enhance user experiences, drive conversions, and achieve e-commerce excellence.

Personalized Product Recommendations: AI-powered product recommendation engines enable businesses to deliver hyper-personalized experiences tailored to the unique preferences and behaviors of individual customers. By analyzing historical data, browsing patterns, and purchase history, AI algorithms can generate personalized product recommendations that resonate with each customer on a deeper level. Through AI-driven recommendations, businesses can increase cross-selling opportunities, boost average order values, and drive repeat purchases, fostering long-term customer loyalty and satisfaction.

Dynamic Content Generation: AI enables businesses to create dynamic and engaging content that adapts in real-time based on user interactions and behaviors. Through machine learning algorithms, AI can optimize content elements such as images, headlines, and calls-to-action to maximize engagement and drive conversions. By leveraging AI-driven content generation tools, businesses can create personalized landing pages, product descriptions, and promotional banners that resonate with target audiences and inspire action.

Automated Design Optimization:

AI streamlines the process of design optimization by automating repetitive tasks, identifying areas for improvement, and implementing changes dynamically based on performance metrics. Through machine learning algorithms, AI can analyze user interactions, heatmaps, and conversion funnels to identify friction points and opportunities for enhancement within Shopify designs. By automating design optimization processes, businesses can iterate rapidly, uncover insights, and refine design elements to create more compelling and effective user experiences.

Predictive Analytics for Conversion Optimization:

AI-driven predictive analytics empower businesses to anticipate user behavior, optimize conversion funnels, and drive meaningful engagement on Shopify storefronts. By analyzing historical data, user interactions, and contextual signals, AI algorithms can forecast future trends, identify potential bottlenecks, and optimize conversion paths to maximize conversion rates and revenue. Through predictive analytics, businesses can gain deeper insights into user behavior, optimize marketing campaigns, and drive more targeted and effective customer engagement strategies.

Enhanced Customer Support and Engagement:

AI-powered chatbots and virtual assistants provide businesses with scalable and cost-effective solutions to deliver personalized customer support and engagement across multiple channels. By leveraging natural language processing (NLP) and machine learning algorithms, chatbots can engage customers in real-time conversations, answer inquiries, resolve issues, and facilitate transactions seamlessly. Through AI-driven customer support, businesses can improve response times, enhance satisfaction levels, and deliver seamless and personalized experiences that drive customer loyalty and retention.

In summary, the integration of AI into Shopify design offers a wealth of opportunities for businesses to enhance user experiences, drive conversions, and achieve e-commerce excellence. By leveraging AI-driven insights, automation, and personalization, businesses can create compelling and immersive storefronts that resonate with customers and inspire action. In the pages that follow, we delve deeper into the practical applications of AI in Shopify design, exploring how innovative technologies and forward-thinking strategies can revolutionize the way businesses connect with customers and achieve e-commerce success.

AI-Powered Product Recommendations

In the ever-evolving landscape of e-commerce, AI-powered product recommendations represent a game-changing approach to enhancing user experiences, driving conversions, and fostering long-term customer loyalty. By harnessing the power of Artificial Intelligence (AI) algorithms, businesses can deliver hyper-personalized recommendations tailored to the unique preferences and behaviors of individual customers, transforming browsing sessions into engaging and inspiring journeys of discovery.

Personalization at Scale: AI-powered product recommendation engines enable businesses to deliver personalized experiences at scale, leveraging vast datasets encompassing customer interactions, browsing history, and purchase patterns. By analyzing historical data and user behaviors, AI algorithms can generate recommendations that resonate with each customer on a deeper level, driving engagement and inspiring action.

Contextual Relevance: AI algorithms take into account a myriad of contextual factors, including past purchases, browsing history, demographic information, and real-time interactions, to generate recommendations that are contextually relevant and timely. By understanding the unique preferences and needs of individual customers, AI-powered recommendation engines can surface products that align with their interests and intentions, enhancing the relevance and effectiveness of product recommendations.

Dynamic Adaptation: AI-powered recommendation engines continuously adapt and evolve based on user feedback and changing preferences, ensuring that recommendations remain relevant and

effective over time. Through machine learning algorithms, recommendation engines can analyze user interactions and feedback to refine and optimize recommendation algorithms, improving the accuracy and effectiveness of product recommendations with each interaction.

Cross-Selling and Upselling Opportunities:

AI-powered recommendation engines enable businesses to identify cross-selling and upselling opportunities by analyzing patterns and associations between products. By analyzing purchase history and product relationships, AI algorithms can identify complementary products and accessories that customers may be interested in, driving incremental sales and maximizing revenue opportunities.

Enhanced User Engagement:

Personalized product recommendations create more engaging and immersive browsing experiences for users, capturing their attention and encouraging exploration. By surfacing relevant products and recommendations, businesses can keep users engaged and invested in the shopping experience, increasing time spent on site and reducing bounce rates.

Increased Conversion Rates: AI-powered product recommendations have been shown to significantly increase conversion rates and average order values by presenting users with products that align with their interests and preferences. By leveraging AI algorithms to surface relevant and compelling recommendations, businesses can inspire users to make purchase decisions and drive more conversions.

Long-Term Customer Loyalty: By delivering personalized and relevant product recommendations, businesses can foster long-term customer loyalty and satisfaction. Personalized recommendations create a sense of value and understanding, demonstrating that the business understands and cares about the needs and preferences of its customers. As a result, customers are more likely to return to the site for future purchases and recommend the brand to others, driving repeat business and word-of-mouth referrals.

In summary, AI-powered product recommendations represent a powerful tool for businesses to enhance user experiences, drive conversions, and foster long-term customer loyalty in the competitive landscape of e-commerce. By leveraging the capabilities of AI algorithms, businesses can deliver personalized and contextually relevant recommendations that resonate with individual customers, transforming browsing sessions into engaging and rewarding experiences.

Personalized User Experience through AI

In the dynamic landscape of e-commerce, delivering a personalized user experience has become paramount to driving engagement, conversions, and long-term customer loyalty. With the advent of Artificial Intelligence (AI) technologies, businesses can now harness the power of data-driven insights and predictive analytics to create hyper-personalized experiences that resonate with individual customers on a deeper level. In the pages that follow, we explore how AI can revolutionize the e-commerce landscape by enabling businesses to deliver personalized user experiences through Shopify design.

Understanding Customer Preferences:

AI algorithms analyze vast datasets encompassing customer interactions, browsing history, purchase patterns, and demographic information to gain insights into individual preferences and behaviors. By understanding the unique preferences and needs of each customer, businesses can tailor their Shopify design to deliver relevant content, product recommendations, and promotional offers that resonate with their target audience.

Dynamic Content Customization:

AI enables businesses to create dynamic and engaging content that adapts in real-time based on user interactions and behaviors. Through machine learning algorithms, AI can optimize content elements such as images, headlines, and calls-to-action to maximize engagement and drive conversions. By delivering personalized content that aligns with user interests and intentions, businesses can create more compelling and relevant user experiences that inspire action.

Contextual Relevance:

AI algorithms take into account a myriad of contextual factors, including user location, device type, time of day, and browsing history, to deliver content and recommendations that are contextually relevant and timely. By leveraging contextual data, businesses can create user experiences that are tailored to the specific needs and preferences of each user, increasing relevance and engagement across the Shopify platform.

Predictive Insights and Recommendations:

AI-powered predictive analytics enable businesses to anticipate user behavior, preferences, and needs based on historical data and user interactions. By analyzing patterns and trends, AI algorithms can predict future actions and preferences, allowing businesses to proactively deliver personalized recommendations, promotions, and content that align with user interests and intentions.

Seamless Multichannel Experiences: AI-powered personalization extends beyond the confines of the Shopify platform, enabling businesses to deliver seamless and consistent experiences across multiple channels and touchpoints. By leveraging AI-driven insights, businesses can personalize user experiences across websites, mobile apps, social media platforms, and email campaigns, creating a cohesive and integrated experience that enhances brand perception and loyalty.

Optimized Customer Journeys:

By personalizing user experiences at every stage of the customer journey, businesses can guide users through the sales funnel more effectively and drive conversions. AI-powered personalization enables businesses to deliver relevant content, product recommendations, and incentives that move users closer to making a purchase decision, ultimately increasing conversion rates and revenue.

Long-Term Customer Loyalty:

Personalized user experiences create a sense of value and connection between businesses and their customers, fostering long-term loyalty and advocacy. By demonstrating an understanding of customer preferences and needs, businesses can build trust and loyalty over time, leading to repeat purchases, positive reviews, and referrals that drive sustainable growth and success.

In summary, AI-powered personalization holds the key to unlocking new opportunities for businesses to deliver compelling, relevant, and engaging user experiences through Shopify design. By leveraging the capabilities of AI algorithms, businesses can create seamless and personalized experiences that resonate with individual customers, driving engagement, conversions, and long-term loyalty in the competitive landscape of e-commerce. Join us as we explore the transformative potential of AI in Shopify design, where innovation knows no bounds, and the future is ours to shape.

Automated Design Optimization

In the dynamic world of e-commerce, where user experience and visual appeal play pivotal roles in driving engagement and conversions, the concept of automated design optimization stands as a beacon of innovation and efficiency. Through the integration of Artificial Intelligence (AI) technologies, businesses can now streamline the process of design optimization, leveraging data-driven insights and predictive analytics to create compelling and effective Shopify designs that resonate with their target audience. In the pages that follow, we explore how automated design optimization can revolutionize the e-commerce landscape and empower businesses to achieve their goals with greater efficiency and effectiveness.

Data-Driven Insights:

Automated design optimization relies on the analysis of vast datasets encompassing user interactions, conversion metrics, and design elements to gain insights into user behavior and preferences. By leveraging machine learning algorithms, businesses can identify patterns, trends, and correlations within the data, uncovering actionable insights that inform design decisions and strategies.

Continuous Iteration and Improvement:

Automated design optimization enables businesses to iterate rapidly and continuously refine their Shopify designs based on real-time feedback and performance metrics. Through A/B testing, multivariate testing, and predictive analytics, businesses can experiment with different design elements, layouts, and content variations to identify the most effective combinations that drive engagement and conversions.

Identification of Friction Points:

AI-powered design optimization algorithms analyze user interactions, heatmaps, and conversion funnels to identify potential friction points and barriers to conversion within Shopify designs. By pinpointing areas of user dissatisfaction or confusion, businesses can prioritize optimization efforts and implement targeted improvements to enhance the user experience and drive more meaningful interactions.

Automated Content Customization:

AI enables businesses

to automate content customization and personalization based on user preferences, behaviors, and contextual factors. Through dynamic content generation tools and recommendation engines, businesses can deliver personalized product recommendations, curated content, and targeted promotions that resonate with individual users, increasing relevance and engagement across the Shopify platform.

Real-Time Adaptation to User Behavior:
Automated design optimization algorithms adapt in real-time to changes in user behavior, preferences, and market dynamics. By monitoring user interactions and performance metrics, AI algorithms can dynamically adjust design elements, layouts, and content to optimize user experiences and drive conversions. Through continuous monitoring and adaptation, businesses can ensure that their Shopify designs remain relevant, engaging, and effective in a rapidly evolving e-commerce landscape.

Streamlined Design Workflow:
Automated design optimization streamlines the design workflow by automating

repetitive tasks and providing actionable insights that inform design decisions. By leveraging AI-powered design tools and platforms, businesses can accelerate the design process, reduce manual effort, and focus their resources on strategic initiatives that drive business growth and success.

Optimized Conversion Paths: AI-powered design optimization enables businesses to optimize conversion paths and user journeys within Shopify designs. By analyzing user behavior and engagement patterns, AI algorithms can identify optimal pathways that guide users through the sales funnel more effectively and drive conversions. Through strategic design optimization, businesses can reduce friction, eliminate barriers, and create seamless and intuitive user experiences that inspire action.

In summary, automated design optimization represents a powerful tool for businesses to enhance user experiences, drive conversions, and achieve e-commerce success on the Shopify platform. By leveraging the capabilities of AI algorithms, businesses can streamline the design process, gain deeper insights into user behavior, and create compelling and effective Shopify designs that resonate with their target audience.

Predictive Analytics for Sales and Customer Behavior:

In the fast-paced world of e-commerce, staying ahead of the curve requires more than just reacting to trends it demands the ability to anticipate customer needs, forecast sales trends, and optimize business strategies in real-time. Predictive analytics, powered by Artificial Intelligence (AI), empowers businesses to do just that by leveraging historical data, machine learning algorithms, and advanced statistical models to predict future outcomes and drive informed decision-making. In the pages that follow, we explore how predictive analytics can revolutionize the e-commerce landscape by enabling businesses to gain deeper insights into sales trends and customer behavior on the Shopify platform.

Forecasting Sales Trends:

Predictive analytics enables businesses to forecast sales trends and identify patterns in purchasing behavior based on historical data and market dynamics. By analyzing factors such as seasonality, promotional activities, and consumer preferences, AI algorithms can generate accurate sales forecasts that inform inventory management, resource allocation, and strategic planning. Through predictive analytics, businesses can anticipate fluctuations in demand, optimize product availability, and capitalize on opportunities for growth and profitability.

Segmentation and Targeting:

Predictive analytics enables businesses to segment customers based on their behavior, preferences, and purchase history, allowing for more targeted and personalized marketing campaigns. By leveraging machine learning algorithms, businesses can identify high-value customer segments, understand their unique needs and preferences, and tailor marketing messages and promotions to resonate with each segment. Through targeted segmentation and personalized targeting, businesses can increase engagement, drive conversions, and foster long-term customer loyalty.

Churn Prediction and Retention Strategies:

Predictive analytics can help businesses identify customers who are at risk of churning and implement proactive retention strategies to minimize churn rates and maximize customer lifetime value. By analyzing patterns in customer behavior, engagement metrics, and demographic information, AI algorithms can predict the likelihood of churn and identify the key factors contributing to customer attrition. Through targeted retention efforts, such as personalized offers, loyalty incentives, and re-engagement campaigns, businesses can reduce churn rates, increase customer loyalty, and maximize revenue potential.

Product Recommendations and Cross-Selling Opportunities:

Predictive analytics enables businesses to generate personalized product recommendations and identify cross-selling opportunities based on historical data and user behavior. By analyzing purchase history, browsing patterns, and product relationships, AI algorithms can identify complementary products and accessories that customers may be interested in, driving incremental sales and maximizing revenue opportunities. Through targeted product recommendations and cross-selling strategies, businesses can increase average order values, boost sales, and enhance the overall shopping experience for customers.

Optimized Pricing Strategies:
Predictive analytics can help businesses optimize pricing strategies by analyzing market trends, competitor pricing, and customer preferences. By leveraging machine learning algorithms, businesses can identify optimal price points, forecast demand elasticity, and adjust pricing dynamically to maximize revenue and profitability. Through data-driven pricing optimization, businesses can stay competitive, capture market share, and drive sustainable growth in the ever-evolving e-commerce landscape.

Fraud Detection and Risk Management: Predictive analytics can

help businesses mitigate the risk of fraud and identify suspicious activities by analyzing transaction data, user behavior, and historical patterns. By leveraging machine learning algorithms, businesses can detect anomalies, identify potential fraudulent transactions, and implement proactive measures to prevent fraud before it occurs. Through predictive analytics, businesses can minimize financial losses, protect sensitive customer information, and maintain trust and credibility among their customer base.

In summary, predictive analytics represents a powerful tool for businesses to gain deeper insights into sales trends and customer behavior, driving informed decision-making and strategic planning on the Shopify platform. By leveraging the capabilities of AI algorithms, businesses can forecast sales trends, identify high-value customer segments, optimize pricing strategies, and implement targeted marketing campaigns that drive growth and profitability.

CHAPTER 4

IMPLEMENTING AI TOOLS AND TECHNIQUES IN SHOPIFY

In the ever-evolving landscape of e-commerce, leveraging Artificial Intelligence (AI) tools and techniques has become essential for businesses seeking to stay competitive, drive engagement, and optimize user experiences on the Shopify platform. By harnessing the power of AI-driven insights, automation, and personalization, businesses can unlock new opportunities to connect with customers, drive conversions, and achieve e-commerce excellence. In the pages that follow, we explore how businesses can implement AI tools and techniques in Shopify to elevate their online storefronts and unlock new avenues for growth and success.

AI-Powered Product Recommendations:

Implementing AI-powered product recommendation engines enables businesses to deliver personalized product recommendations tailored to the unique preferences and behaviors of individual customers. By integrating AI algorithms into the Shopify platform, businesses can analyze customer interactions, browsing history, and purchase patterns to generate relevant and compelling product recommendations that drive engagement and conversions.

Dynamic Content Customization:

AI enables businesses to automate content customization and personalization based on user preferences, behaviors, and contextual factors. By leveraging AI-driven content generation tools and recommendation engines, businesses can deliver personalized content, product descriptions, and promotional offers that resonate with individual users, increasing relevance and engagement across the Shopify platform.

Automated Design Optimization:

Integrating AI-powered design optimization tools into Shopify enables businesses to streamline the process of design optimization and create compelling and effective user experiences. By leveraging

AI algorithms to analyze user interactions, heatmaps, and conversion funnels, businesses can identify areas for improvement within their Shopify designs and implement targeted optimizations that enhance user engagement and drive conversions.

Predictive Analytics for Sales and Customer Behavior:

Implementing predictive analytics tools enables businesses to gain deeper insights into sales trends and customer behavior on the Shopify platform. By analyzing historical data, market trends, and user interactions, businesses can forecast sales trends, identify high-value customer segments, and optimize marketing strategies to drive growth and profitability.

Automated Customer Support and Engagement:

Integrating AI-powered chatbots and virtual assistants into Shopify enables businesses to deliver personalized customer support and engagement across multiple channels. By leveraging natural language processing (NLP) and machine learning algorithms, businesses can automate responses to customer inquiries, resolve issues, and facilitate transactions seamlessly, enhancing the overall customer experience and driving satisfaction.

Real-Time Data Analysis and Insights:

Implementing AI-driven analytics tools enables businesses to analyze real-time data and gain actionable insights into user behavior, performance metrics, and market trends on the Shopify platform. By leveraging AI algorithms to analyze vast datasets, businesses can identify patterns, trends, and correlations within the data, uncovering opportunities for optimization and growth.

Integration with Third-Party AI Solutions:

Shopify's open architecture allows businesses to integrate with third-party AI solutions and platforms, expanding their capabilities and unlocking new functionalities. By leveraging APIs and integration tools, businesses can seamlessly incorporate AI-powered features and services into their Shopify storefronts, enhancing the user experience and driving business outcomes.

In summary, implementing AI tools and techniques in Shopify empowers businesses to create more compelling, personalized, and effective user experiences that drive engagement, conversions, and long-term customer loyalty. By harnessing the power of AI-driven insights, automation, and personalization, businesses can unlock new opportunities for growth and success in the competitive landscape of e-commerce.

Choosing the Right AI Tools for Shopify Design

In the rapidly evolving landscape of e-commerce, selecting the right AI tools for Shopify design is paramount to creating compelling user experiences, driving engagement, and maximizing conversions. With a myriad of AI-powered solutions available, businesses must carefully evaluate their needs, objectives, and technical requirements to identify the tools and techniques that best align with their goals. In the pages that follow, we explore key considerations and best practices for choosing the right AI tools for Shopify design and unlocking new opportunities for growth and success.

Define Your Objectives: Before embarking on the journey of selecting AI tools for Shopify design, it's essential to define clear objectives and outcomes that align with your business goals. Whether your focus is on enhancing user experiences, driving conversions, or optimizing operational efficiency, articulating your objectives will help guide the selection process and ensure that the chosen tools align with your strategic priorities.

Assess Your Technical Requirements: Consideration of your technical requirements is crucial when choosing AI tools for Shopify design. Evaluate factors such as scalability, integration capabilities, and technical support to ensure that the selected tools can seamlessly integrate with your existing infrastructure and meet your business needs both now and in the future. Assessing technical requirements upfront will help avoid potential compatibility issues and streamline the implementation process.

Understand Your Data Needs: AI-powered solutions rely on data to generate insights, make predictions, and drive informed decision-making. Evaluate your data sources, quality, and accessibility to ensure that the selected AI tools have access to the necessary data inputs to deliver meaningful results. Consideration of data privacy and security requirements is also essential to safeguard sensitive customer information and comply with regulatory standards.

Evaluate AI Capabilities: Different AI tools offer varying capabilities and functionalities depending on their underlying algorithms and models. Evaluate the AI capabilities of each tool, such as machine learning, natural language processing, computer vision, and predictive analytics, to determine which features are most relevant to your Shopify design objectives. Choose tools that offer a comprehensive suite of AI capabilities tailored to your specific use cases and requirements.

Consider User Experience and Usability: The effectiveness of AI tools for Shopify design depends not only on their technical capabilities but also on their user experience and usability. Consider factors such as ease of use, intuitive interface design, and accessibility features to ensure that the selected tools can be effectively utilized by your team members across different skill levels and backgrounds. A user-friendly interface and streamlined workflow will facilitate adoption and maximize the value of the AI tools in your Shopify design process.

Explore Integration and Customization Options: Integration capabilities and customization options are key considerations when choosing AI tools for Shopify design. Evaluate whether the selected tools offer seamless integration with the Shopify platform and support customization to align with your branding and design requirements. Explore whether the tools provide APIs, SDKs, or developer tools that enable further customization and integration with third-party systems and services.

Seek Recommendations and Reviews:

Before making a final decision, seek recommendations and reviews from industry experts, peers, and trusted sources to gain insights into the performance, reliability, and effectiveness of the AI tools under consideration. Consider factors such as user testimonials, case studies, and third-party evaluations to assess the track record and reputation of the AI tools and vendors in the market.

Trial and Pilot Programs:

Many AI vendors offer trial and pilot programs that allow businesses to test drive their tools and evaluate their suitability for Shopify design projects. Take advantage of these opportunities to assess the performance, functionality, and fit of the AI tools within your specific use case and environment. Engage with vendors directly to discuss your requirements, objectives, and expectations, and leverage their expertise to make informed decisions.

In summary, choosing the right AI tools for Shopify design requires careful consideration of objectives, technical requirements, data needs, AI capabilities, user experience, integration options, and vendor reputation. By following best practices and evaluating each tool against these criteria, businesses can select the AI tools that best align with their goals and empower them to create compelling, personalized, and effective user experiences on the Shopify platform.

Integrating AI Applications with Shopify

In the dynamic landscape of e-commerce, integrating Artificial Intelligence (AI) applications with Shopify represents a transformative opportunity for businesses to enhance user experiences, drive conversions, and unlock new avenues for growth and success. By leveraging the power of AI-driven insights, automation, and personalization, businesses can create compelling and effective Shopify storefronts that resonate with their target audience and drive meaningful engagement. In the pages that follow, we explore best practices and considerations for integrating AI applications with Shopify and harnessing the full potential of AI to empower e-commerce excellence.

Identify Use Cases and Objectives: Before embarking on the integration of AI applications with Shopify, it's essential to identify clear use cases and objectives that align with your business goals. Whether your focus is on personalizing user experiences, optimizing product recommendations, or automating customer support, articulating your objectives will help guide the integration process and ensure that AI applications deliver tangible value to your Shopify storefront.

Evaluate AI Solutions: Explore the diverse landscape of AI solutions available and evaluate each solution based on its capabilities, features, and compatibility with Shopify. Consider factors such as machine learning algorithms, natural language processing capabilities, and predictive analytics tools to determine which AI solutions best address your specific use cases and requirements.

Assess Integration Options: Shopify offers various integration options to seamlessly incorporate AI applications into your storefront. Explore Shopify's App

71

Store, developer tools, and APIs to identify integration options that align with your technical requirements and preferences. Evaluate the ease of integration, documentation, and support provided by AI vendors to ensure a smooth and seamless integration process.

Customize and Configure: Tailor AI applications to meet the unique needs and branding requirements of your Shopify storefront. Leverage customization options and configuration settings to align AI applications with your brand identity, design aesthetics, and user experience goals. Ensure that AI applications seamlessly blend into your Shopify environment and enhance the overall look and feel of your storefront.

Data Integration and Privacy: Consider data integration and privacy implications when integrating AI applications with Shopify. Ensure that AI applications have access to the necessary data inputs, such as customer interactions, purchase history, and product catalog, to generate meaningful insights and recommendations. Implement data governance measures and security protocols to protect sensitive customer information and comply with regulatory standards.

Test and Iterate: Conduct thorough testing and validation of AI applications within your Shopify environment to ensure functionality, performance, and reliability. Leverage testing frameworks, user feedback, and analytics tools to identify areas for improvement and iterate on AI applications iteratively. Solicit feedback from users and stakeholders to gauge the effectiveness and impact of AI applications on user experiences and business outcomes.

Monitor and Optimize: Continuously monitor the performance and impact of AI applications on your Shopify storefront and user engagement metrics. Leverage analytics dashboards, KPIs, and performance metrics to track key indicators such as conversion rates, average order value, and customer satisfaction. Identify trends, patterns, and opportunities for optimization, and fine-

tune AI applications to maximize their effectiveness and value over time.

Stay Abreast of Emerging Trends:
The field of AI is rapidly evolving, with new advancements, techniques, and algorithms emerging at a rapid pace. Stay abreast of industry trends, research developments, and best practices in AI to ensure that your Shopify storefront remains at the forefront of innovation and technology. Explore opportunities to leverage emerging AI technologies, such as deep learning, reinforcement learning, and natural language understanding, to enhance user experiences and drive business growth.

In summary, integrating AI applications with Shopify offers businesses a unique opportunity to enhance user experiences, drive conversions, and unlock new opportunities for growth and innovation. By following best practices and considerations for integration, businesses can harness the full potential of AI to create compelling, personalized, and effective Shopify storefronts that resonate with their target audience and drive meaningful engagement.

Customizing AI Solutions for Specific E-Commerce Needs

In the dynamic landscape of e-commerce, businesses often encounter unique challenges and opportunities that require tailored solutions to address specific needs and objectives. Customizing Artificial Intelligence (AI) solutions for e-commerce allows businesses to harness the full potential of AI technologies to optimize user experiences, drive conversions, and unlock new avenues for growth and innovation. In the pages that follow, we explore best practices and considerations for customizing AI solutions to meet specific e-commerce needs and empower businesses to achieve their goals on the Shopify platform.

Identify Key Business Objectives:

Before customizing AI solutions for e-commerce, it's essential to identify key business objectives and strategic priorities that align with your organization's goals. Whether your focus is on increasing sales, enhancing user experiences, or improving operational efficiency, articulating clear objectives will help guide the customization process and ensure that AI solutions deliver tangible value to your e-commerce initiatives.

Understand User Behavior and Preferences:

Gain a deep understanding of user behavior, preferences, and pain points within your e-commerce ecosystem. Analyze customer interactions, browsing patterns, and purchase history to identify opportunities for customization and personalization. Leverage AI-driven analytics tools to gain actionable insights into user behavior and preferences, informing customization strategies that resonate with your target audience.

Evaluate AI Capabilities and Features:

Evaluate the capabilities and features of AI solutions to determine their suitability for addressing specific e-commerce needs and objectives. Consider factors such as machine learning algorithms, natural language processing capabilities, and predictive analytics tools to identify solutions that align with your customization requirements. Choose AI solutions that offer flexibility, scalability, and customization options tailored to your e-commerce ecosystem.

Define Customization Requirements:

Define specific customization requirements and use cases that align with your e-commerce needs and objectives. Whether you're looking to personalize product recommendations, optimize pricing strategies, or automate customer support, clearly define the scope, objectives, and success criteria for customization initiatives. Collaborate with cross-functional teams, including marketing, sales, and IT, to ensure alignment and buy-in for customization efforts.

Leverage AI APIs and Developer Tools:

Many AI vendors offer APIs, SDKs, and developer tools that enable businesses to customize and extend AI solutions to meet their specific needs. Leverage these tools to integrate AI capabilities seamlessly into your e-commerce platform and tailor them to address unique business requirements. Explore customization options such as model training, feature engineering, and algorithm tuning to optimize AI solutions for your specific use cases.

Data Integration and Model Training: Ensure seamless integration of AI solutions with your e-commerce data infrastructure to access relevant data inputs and generate meaningful insights. Integrate customer data, transaction history, product catalog, and other relevant datasets to train AI models and algorithms effectively. Implement data governance measures and security protocols to protect sensitive customer information and comply with regulatory standards.

Iterate and Iterate: Customization is an iterative process that requires continuous experimentation, iteration, and optimization. Leverage agile methodologies and iterative development practices to iteratively refine and enhance AI solutions based on user feedback and performance metrics. Monitor key performance indicators (KPIs) such as conversion rates, average order value, and customer

satisfaction to gauge the effectiveness of customization efforts and prioritize optimization initiatives accordingly.

Stay Agile and Adaptive: The e-commerce landscape is constantly evolving, with new trends, technologies, and customer expectations emerging at a rapid pace. Stay agile and adaptive in your approach to customization, anticipating changes and proactively adapting AI solutions to address evolving needs and challenges. Stay abreast of industry trends, research developments, and best practices in AI to leverage new opportunities and stay ahead of the curve.

In summary, customizing AI solutions for specific e-commerce needs empowers businesses to optimize user experiences, drive conversions, and unlock new opportunities for growth and innovation on the Shopify platform. By following best practices and considerations for customization, businesses can tailor AI solutions to address unique business requirements and achieve their goals in the competitive e-commerce landscape.

CHAPTER 5

CASE STUDIES AND EXAMPLES

Successful Implementation of AI in Shopify Design

Implementing Artificial Intelligence (AI) in Shopify design represents a transformative opportunity for businesses to elevate user experiences, drive conversions, and unlock new avenues for growth and innovation. In this section, we delve into key strategies and best practices for the successful implementation of AI in Shopify design, empowering businesses to harness the full potential of AI technologies and achieve e-commerce excellence.

Define Clear Objectives and Use Cases

Before embarking on the implementation of AI in Shopify design, define clear objectives and use cases that align with your business goals and strategic priorities.

Identify specific areas within your Shopify storefront where AI can add value, such as personalized product recommendations, dynamic content customization, or automated customer support.

Select the Right AI Tools and Technologies:

Evaluate a diverse range of AI tools and technologies to identify solutions that best align with your customization requirements, technical capabilities, and user experience goals.

Choose AI solutions that offer scalability, flexibility, and customization options tailored to your specific needs and objectives.

Integrate Seamlessly with Shopify:

Leverage Shopify's open architecture and integration capabilities to seamlessly incorporate AI solutions into your storefront.

Explore Shopify's App Store, developer tools, and APIs to identify integration options that align with your technical requirements and preferences.

Customize and Tailor AI Solutions:

Customize AI solutions to meet the unique needs and branding requirements of your Shopify storefront.

Leverage customization options and configuration settings to align AI solutions with your brand identity, design aesthetics, and user experience goals.

Ensure Data Integration and Privacy:

Ensure seamless integration of AI solutions with your e-commerce data infrastructure to access relevant data inputs and generate meaningful insights.

Implement robust data governance measures and security protocols to protect sensitive customer information and comply with regulatory standards.

Train and Optimize AI Models:

Train AI models and algorithms using high-quality data to ensure accuracy, reliability, and effectiveness.

Continuously monitor performance metrics and user feedback to identify areas for optimization and refinement, iterating on AI models iteratively to enhance performance over time.

Provide Adequate Training and Support:

Provide adequate training and support to your team members to ensure effective utilization of AI solutions within your Shopify environment.

Offer training programs, resources, and documentation to empower team members with the knowledge and skills required to leverage AI effectively in their day-to-day activities.

Measure and Evaluate Performance:

Establish key performance indicators (KPIs) and metrics to measure the performance and impact of AI in Shopify design.

Monitor user engagement metrics, conversion rates, and customer satisfaction scores to gauge the effectiveness of AI solutions and identify opportunities for improvement.

Iterate and Innovate Continuously:

Embrace a culture of continuous innovation and iteration, proactively exploring new AI technologies, trends, and best practices.

Stay abreast of industry developments and user feedback, iterating on AI solutions iteratively to address evolving needs and challenges in the competitive landscape of e-commerce.

By following these strategies and best practices, businesses can successfully implement AI in Shopify design, unlocking new opportunities for growth, innovation, and e-commerce excellence. Join us as we explore the transformative potential of AI in Shopify design, where innovation knows no bounds, and the future is ours to shape.

Real-life Examples of AI-driven E-commerce Growth

In the realm of e-commerce, businesses across various industries have embraced AI-driven technologies to propel growth, enhance user experiences, and achieve remarkable success on platforms like Shopify. Here are some real-life examples of AI-driven e-commerce growth that illustrate the transformative power of AI in Shopify design:

Amazon's Product Recommendations:

Amazon, the global e-commerce giant, leverages sophisticated AI algorithms to power its product recommendation engine.

By analyzing vast amounts of customer data, including browsing history, purchase behavior, and demographic information, Amazon's AI-driven recommendation engine suggests relevant products to users, driving cross-selling opportunities and increasing average order value.

Amazon's personalized product recommendations have contributed significantly to its e-commerce growth, fostering customer loyalty and driving repeat purchases on its platform.

Netflix's Content Personalization:

Netflix, a leading streaming service, employs AI-driven algorithms to personalize content recommendations for its users.

By analyzing viewing habits, engagement metrics, and user preferences, Netflix's AI-powered recommendation engine suggests movies and TV shows tailored to each user's tastes and interests.

Netflix's personalized content recommendations have played a pivotal role in driving user engagement, reducing churn rates, and fueling the company's growth in the competitive streaming market.

Sephora's Virtual Artist:

Sephora, a renowned beauty retailer, integrates AI technologies into its e-commerce platform to enhance the online shopping experience for its customers.

Sephora's Virtual Artist tool utilizes augmented reality (AR) and AI algorithms to enable customers to virtually try on makeup products and experiment with different looks in real-time.

Sephora's AI-driven Virtual Artist has driven significant e-commerce growth by increasing user engagement, reducing purchase hesitation, and driving conversions on its platform.

Pinterest's Visual Search:

Pinterest, a popular visual discovery platform, harnesses AI-driven visual search technologies to enhance user experiences and drive e-commerce growth.

Pinterest's visual search feature enables users to discover products and ideas by uploading images or using the camera to search for visually similar items on the platform.

Pinterest's AI-powered visual search has transformed the way users discover and shop for products, driving e-commerce growth by connecting users with relevant products and inspiring purchase decisions.

Walmart's Inventory Management:

Walmart, a leading retail corporation, utilizes AI-driven technologies to optimize inventory management and supply chain operations across its e-commerce platform.

Walmart's AI algorithms analyze historical sales data, market trends, and external factors to forecast demand, optimize stock levels, and minimize out-of-stock situations.

Walmart's AI-powered inventory management system has enhanced operational efficiency, reduced costs, and driven e-commerce growth by ensuring product availability and customer satisfaction on its platform.

These real-life examples demonstrate the transformative impact of AI-driven technologies on e-commerce growth, illustrating how businesses leverage AI to enhance user experiences, drive conversions, and achieve success on platforms like Shopify. By embracing innovation and harnessing the power of AI, businesses can unlock new opportunities for growth, innovation, and e-commerce excellence in the competitive digital landscape.

Lessons Learned from Case Studies

The case studies presented in the realm of e-commerce, particularly in the integration of AI within Shopify design, offer invaluable insights and lessons that illuminate the path to success for businesses seeking to harness the power of AI in their online ventures. Here are some key lessons learned from these case studies:

Personalization Drives Engagement and Conversions:

Personalized experiences significantly enhance user engagement and drive conversions in e-commerce platforms like Shopify.

AI-powered recommendation engines, personalized content, and targeted marketing campaigns tailored to individual preferences and behaviors lead to higher levels of customer satisfaction and loyalty.

Data is the Foundation of AI Success:

The quality and quantity of data play a crucial role in the effectiveness of AI-driven solutions.

Businesses must prioritize data collection, management, and analysis to fuel AI algorithms and generate meaningful insights that drive informed decision-making and personalized experiences.

User Experience is Paramount:

Seamless user experiences are essential for the success of AI-driven e-commerce initiatives.

Businesses must prioritize intuitive interface design, streamlined workflows, and responsive customer support to create frictionless experiences that delight users and foster long-term relationships.

Continuous Iteration and Optimization are Key:

E-commerce is an ever-evolving landscape, and successful AI implementations require continuous iteration and optimization.

Businesses must monitor performance metrics, gather user feedback, and iterate on AI solutions iteratively to address evolving needs, preferences, and challenges in the competitive e-commerce market.

Transparency and Trust are Critical:

Transparency and trust are foundational principles for successful AI implementations.

Businesses must be transparent about data collection practices, privacy policies, and AI-driven algorithms to build trust with users and foster a positive perception of AI technologies in e-commerce environments.

Collaboration across Teams is Essential:

Successful AI implementations require collaboration across diverse teams and disciplines within the organization.

Marketing, sales, IT, and customer service teams must work together to define objectives, implement AI solutions, and optimize user experiences in alignment with business goals and strategic priorities.

Adaptability and Innovation are Imperative:

The e-commerce landscape is characterized by rapid technological advancements and shifting consumer preferences.

Businesses must remain adaptable and innovative, embracing emerging AI technologies, trends, and best practices to stay ahead of the curve and drive sustained

91

growth and competitiveness in the dynamic e-commerce market.

By internalizing these lessons learned from case studies, businesses can navigate the complexities of AI integration in Shopify design with confidence, clarity, and purpose, unlocking new opportunities for growth, innovation, and e-commerce excellence.

CHAPTER 6

CHALLENGES AND CONSIDERATIONS

Integrating AI into Shopify design offers immense potential for businesses to enhance user experiences, drive conversions, and achieve e-commerce success. However, this transformative journey is not without its challenges and considerations. Here are some key challenges and considerations that businesses should be mindful of when harnessing AI for Shopify design:

Data Quality and Accessibility:

Challenge: AI algorithms require access to high-quality, relevant data to generate meaningful insights and recommendations. However, ensuring data quality and accessibility can be challenging, especially when dealing with disparate data sources and formats.

Consideration: Businesses must prioritize data governance, data management, and data integration initiatives to ensure that AI algorithms have access to the necessary data inputs. Implementing data quality checks, data cleansing processes, and data security measures can help maintain data integrity and reliability.

Algorithm Bias and Fairness:

Challenge: AI algorithms may inadvertently exhibit bias or discrimination, leading to unfair or inequitable outcomes for certain user groups.

Consideration: Businesses must be vigilant in monitoring AI algorithms for bias and fairness, conducting regular audits and assessments to identify and mitigate potential biases. Implementing transparency measures, fairness assessments, and diversity considerations can help ensure that AI-driven solutions promote equitable experiences for all users.

Privacy and Data Security:

Challenge: Collecting and processing user data for AI-driven applications raises concerns around privacy and data security.

Consideration: Businesses must prioritize user privacy and data security by implementing robust data protection measures, obtaining user consent for data collection and processing, and complying with relevant data protection regulations such as GDPR and CCPA. Implementing encryption, access controls, and data anonymization techniques can help safeguard sensitive customer information and build trust with users.

Integration Complexity and Technical Challenges:

Challenge: Integrating AI technologies into the Shopify platform may pose technical challenges and complexities, particularly for businesses with limited technical expertise or resources.

Consideration: Businesses must carefully evaluate their technical requirements, capabilities, and constraints when selecting AI solutions for Shopify design. Collaborating with experienced developers, leveraging third-party integrations, and exploring plug-and-play AI solutions can help simplify the integration process and mitigate technical challenges.

User Adoption and Acceptance:

Challenge: User adoption and acceptance of AI-driven features and functionalities may vary among different user segments, leading to resistance or skepticism.

Consideration: Businesses must prioritize user education, communication, and engagement strategies to promote awareness and acceptance of AI-driven features. Providing clear explanations of AI capabilities, soliciting user feedback, and offering user-friendly interfaces can help increase user adoption and satisfaction.

Cost and Resource Allocation:

Challenge: Implementing AI technologies in Shopify design may require significant investments in terms of financial resources, time, and expertise.

Consideration: Businesses must conduct thorough cost-benefit analyses and resource assessments to evaluate the feasibility and ROI of AI implementations. Exploring flexible pricing models, seeking government grants or incentives, and partnering with AI vendors or service providers can help mitigate cost considerations and optimize resource allocation.

Ethical and Legal Implications:

Challenge: AI implementations in e-commerce raise complex ethical and legal considerations, including issues related to accountability, transparency, and liability.

Consideration: Businesses must adhere to ethical principles, industry standards, and regulatory requirements governing the responsible use of AI technologies. Implementing ethical guidelines, conducting impact assessments, and fostering a culture of ethical AI governance can help mitigate ethical and legal risks and ensure responsible AI usage in Shopify design.

Navigating these challenges and considerations requires careful planning, collaboration, and ongoing diligence. By addressing these challenges proactively and adopting a holistic approach to AI integration, businesses can unlock the full potential of AI in Shopify design, driving innovation, differentiation, and sustained growth in the competitive e-commerce landscape. Join us as we explore the transformative potential of AI in Shopify design, where innovation knows no bounds, and the future is ours to shape.

Ethical and Privacy Concerns in AI-Driven E-Commerce

As businesses harness the power of Artificial Intelligence (AI) to drive innovation and enhance user experiences in e-commerce, it's imperative to address ethical and privacy concerns associated with AI-driven technologies. In the context of Shopify design and e-commerce platforms, several ethical and privacy considerations emerge:

Data Privacy and Security:

E-commerce platforms collect vast amounts of user data to personalize experiences and drive conversions. However, ensuring the privacy and security of this data is paramount.

Businesses must implement robust data protection measures, including encryption, access controls, and data anonymization techniques, to safeguard sensitive user information from unauthorized access and data breaches.

User Consent and Transparency:

Transparent communication and obtaining user consent are essential components of ethical AI-driven e-commerce.

Businesses must clearly communicate their data collection practices, privacy policies, and the use of AI algorithms to users, empowering them to make informed decisions about their data and online interactions.

Algorithmic Bias and Fairness:

AI algorithms powering e-commerce platforms may inadvertently exhibit bias or discrimination, resulting in unfair or inequitable outcomes for certain user groups.

Businesses must proactively monitor AI algorithms for bias and fairness, conduct regular audits and assessments, and implement mechanisms to mitigate biases and promote equitable experiences for all users.

User Profiling and Targeted Advertising:

AI-driven user profiling and targeted advertising raise concerns about user autonomy, manipulation, and intrusive marketing practices.

Businesses must strike a balance between personalized marketing initiatives and respecting user privacy and autonomy. Implementing granular privacy controls, allowing users to opt-out of targeted advertising, and providing transparency about advertising practices can help mitigate concerns around user profiling.

Impact on Vulnerable Populations:

Vulnerable populations, including children, elderly individuals, and individuals with limited digital literacy, may be disproportionately impacted by AI-driven e-commerce practices.

Businesses must consider the potential impact of AI technologies on vulnerable populations and take proactive steps to mitigate risks, such as providing accessible user interfaces, offering clear guidance and support, and prioritizing user safety and well-being.

Accountability and Responsibility:

With the increasing reliance on AI-driven decision-making in e-commerce, questions of accountability and responsibility become paramount.

Businesses must establish clear lines of accountability for AI-driven systems, define roles and responsibilities for monitoring and oversight, and establish mechanisms for addressing potential harms or unintended consequences arising from AI implementations.

Regulatory Compliance and Legal Frameworks:

E-commerce businesses must comply with relevant regulatory requirements and legal frameworks governing data privacy, consumer protection, and AI ethics.

Businesses must stay abreast of evolving regulatory landscapes, proactively engage with regulatory authorities, and ensure that their AI-driven e-commerce practices align with legal requirements and industry standards.

By addressing these ethical and privacy concerns proactively and adopting a responsible approach to AI-driven e-commerce, businesses can build trust with users, foster positive relationships, and promote ethical innovation in the digital marketplace.

Overcoming Implementation Challenges

The implementation of AI in Shopify design presents businesses with a myriad of challenges that require careful consideration and strategic planning. By addressing these challenges proactively, businesses can navigate the complexities of AI integration and unlock the full potential of AI-driven e-commerce experiences. Here are some strategies for overcoming implementation challenges in the context of "Empowering E-Commerce: Harnessing AI for Shopify Design":

Technical Expertise and Resources:

Challenge: Implementing AI in Shopify design requires technical expertise and resources, which may be limited or inaccessible for some businesses.

Strategy: Businesses can overcome this challenge by investing in talent development, training programs, and strategic partnerships with AI experts and technology providers. Leveraging third-party integrations, pre-built AI solutions, and developer tools offered by Shopify can also streamline the implementation process and reduce technical barriers.

Data Integration and Quality:

Challenge: Integrating AI into Shopify design relies on access to high-quality data from disparate sources, which may be fragmented or inconsistent.

Strategy: Businesses should prioritize data integration initiatives, data cleansing processes, and data quality checks to ensure that AI algorithms have access to reliable data inputs. Collaborating with data analysts, leveraging data management platforms, and implementing data governance frameworks can help streamline data integration efforts and enhance data quality.

User Adoption and Change Management:

Challenge: User adoption of AI-driven features and functionalities in Shopify design may vary among different user segments, requiring effective change management strategies.

Strategy: Businesses should prioritize user education, training, and engagement initiatives to promote awareness and acceptance of AI-driven enhancements. Providing clear explanations of AI capabilities, soliciting user feedback, and offering user-friendly interfaces can help increase user adoption and satisfaction.

Privacy and Security Concerns:

Challenge: Integrating AI into Shopify design raises concerns about data privacy, security, and compliance with regulatory requirements.

Strategy: Businesses must implement robust data protection measures, obtain

104

user consent for data collection and processing, and comply with relevant data privacy regulations such as GDPR and CCPA. Conducting privacy impact assessments, engaging with legal counsel, and implementing encryption and access controls can help mitigate privacy and security risks.

Cost and ROI Considerations:

Challenge: Implementing AI in Shopify design entails financial investments and resource allocations, with uncertain returns on investment (ROI).

Strategy: Businesses should conduct thorough cost-benefit analyses, ROI assessments, and risk evaluations to evaluate the feasibility and potential impact of AI implementations. Exploring flexible pricing models, seeking government grants or incentives, and conducting pilot projects or proof-of-concepts can help mitigate cost considerations and optimize resource allocation.

Ethical and Social Implications:

Challenge: AI implementations in e-commerce raise complex ethical and social considerations, including issues related to algorithmic bias, transparency, and accountability.

Strategy: Businesses must adhere to ethical guidelines, industry standards, and regulatory requirements governing the responsible use of AI technologies. Implementing ethical AI frameworks, fostering a culture of ethical decision-making, and engaging with stakeholders can help address ethical and social implications proactively.

By embracing these strategies and adopting a holistic approach to AI implementation, businesses can overcome implementation challenges and harness the transformative power of AI to drive innovation, differentiation, and e-commerce excellence on the Shopify platform.

Ensuring Data Security and Compliance

In the rapidly evolving landscape of e-commerce, ensuring robust data security and compliance with regulatory requirements is paramount, particularly when integrating AI technologies into Shopify design. By prioritizing data security and compliance, businesses can build trust with users, mitigate risks, and foster a secure and compliant e-commerce environment. Here are key strategies for ensuring data security and compliance in the context of "Empowering E-Commerce: Harnessing AI for Shopify Design":

Comprehensive Data Governance Framework:

Establish a comprehensive data governance framework that outlines policies, procedures, and controls for managing and protecting data throughout its lifecycle.

Define roles and responsibilities for data stewardship, access management, and compliance oversight to ensure accountability and transparency in data management practices.

Data Encryption and Access Controls:

Implement robust encryption mechanisms to protect sensitive data at rest and in transit, safeguarding against unauthorized access and data breaches.

Enforce granular access controls and authentication mechanisms to restrict access to confidential data and ensure that only authorized users can access sensitive information.

Regular Security Audits and Assessments:

Conduct regular security audits, vulnerability assessments, and penetration testing to identify and mitigate security risks and vulnerabilities in Shopify design and AI-driven applications.

Engage third-party security experts and auditors to validate security controls, assess compliance with industry standards, and recommend remediation measures as needed.

Data Minimization and Retention Policies:

Adopt data minimization principles to limit the collection, storage, and retention of personal data to what is necessary for legitimate business purposes.

Define data retention policies and procedures that specify the retention periods for different types of data, ensuring compliance with regulatory requirements and minimizing exposure to data breaches.

User Consent and Transparent Data Practices:

Obtain explicit user consent for data collection, processing, and sharing activities, providing clear explanations of data practices and purposes to users.

Implement transparent data practices, such as privacy notices, consent management tools, and user-friendly interfaces, to empower users to make informed decisions about their data.

Compliance with Regulatory Requirements:

Stay abreast of relevant data protection regulations, such as GDPR, CCPA, and PCI DSS, that govern the collection, processing, and storage of personal and financial data in e-commerce environments.

Conduct regular compliance assessments, review regulatory updates, and adapt data security and privacy practices to ensure alignment with evolving regulatory requirements.

Employee Training and Awareness:

Provide comprehensive training and awareness programs for employees to educate them about data security best practices, regulatory requirements, and the importance of safeguarding sensitive information.

Foster a culture of security awareness and accountability across the organization, encouraging employees to report security incidents, adhere to data security policies, and participate in ongoing training initiatives.

By implementing these strategies and adopting a proactive approach to data security and compliance, businesses can mitigate risks, protect sensitive information, and build trust with users in the competitive landscape of e-commerce.

CHAPTER 7

FUTURE TRENDS AND INNOVATIONS

As e-commerce continues to evolve, fueled by advancements in technology and shifting consumer preferences, businesses must anticipate and embrace emerging trends and innovations to stay ahead of the curve and drive sustained growth in the competitive landscape of online retail. In the context of "Empowering E-Commerce: Harnessing AI for Shopify Design," here are some future trends and innovations that businesses should consider:

AI-Powered Virtual Assistants and Chatbots:

AI-driven virtual assistants and chatbots will play an increasingly prominent role in e-commerce, providing personalized assistance, answering customer inquiries, and facilitating seamless transactions on Shopify platforms.

Future innovations may include enhanced natural language processing capabilities, voice-enabled interactions, and integration with advanced AI technologies to deliver more intuitive and context-aware customer experiences.

Augmented Reality (AR) and Virtual Reality (VR) Experiences:

AR and VR technologies will revolutionize the way consumers shop online, offering immersive and interactive experiences that bridge the gap between the digital and physical worlds.

Future innovations may include virtual try-on experiences, interactive product visualization tools, and AR-powered product demonstrations, enriching the e-commerce journey and driving higher levels of engagement and conversion on Shopify platforms.

Hyper-Personalization and Predictive Analytics:

Hyper-personalization will become increasingly sophisticated, leveraging AI algorithms and predictive analytics to anticipate customer preferences, tailor product recommendations, and deliver personalized marketing messages in real-time.

Future innovations may include dynamic pricing strategies, personalized content curation, and predictive inventory management, enabling businesses to optimize user experiences and drive conversions based on individual customer needs and behaviors.

Voice Commerce and Smart Speaker Integration:

Voice commerce will emerge as a mainstream channel for e-commerce transactions, facilitated by the proliferation of smart speakers and voice-enabled devices.

Future innovations may include voice-activated shopping assistants, voice-controlled checkout processes, and integration with voice search technologies to enable seamless voice-driven interactions and transactions on Shopify platforms.

Blockchain Technology and Decentralized E-Commerce:

Blockchain technology will disrupt traditional e-commerce models by enabling decentralized marketplaces, secure

114

payment processing, and transparent supply chain management.

Future innovations may include blockchain-based smart contracts, tokenized loyalty programs, and decentralized identity solutions, empowering businesses and consumers alike to transact securely and transparently on Shopify platforms.

Sustainable and Ethical E-Commerce Practices:

Sustainable and ethical e-commerce practices will become increasingly important to environmentally and socially conscious consumers, driving demand for eco-friendly products, fair trade practices, and transparent supply chains.

Future innovations may include sustainability certifications, ethical sourcing platforms, and carbon footprint calculators, enabling businesses to showcase their commitment to sustainability and ethics on Shopify platforms.

By embracing these future trends and innovations, businesses can unlock new opportunities for growth, innovation, and e-commerce excellence on Shopify platforms. By staying abreast of emerging technologies, consumer trends, and industry developments, businesses can position themselves as leaders in the evolving landscape of online retail, empowering e-commerce for the future.

Emerging Technologies in E-Commerce and AI:

In the dynamic landscape of e-commerce, emerging technologies are reshaping the way businesses engage with customers, optimize operations, and drive growth. By harnessing the power of Artificial Intelligence (AI) and integrating innovative technologies into Shopify design, businesses can unlock new opportunities for innovation, differentiation, and e-commerce excellence. Here are some emerging technologies in e-commerce and AI that are transforming the future of online retail in the context of "Empowering E-Commerce: Harnessing AI for Shopify Design":

Natural Language Processing (NLP) and Conversational Commerce:

Natural Language Processing (NLP) enables computers to understand, interpret, and generate human language, powering conversational commerce experiences such as chatbots, virtual assistants, and voice-enabled interfaces.

By integrating NLP capabilities into Shopify design, businesses can enhance customer engagement, automate customer support, and facilitate seamless transactions through natural language interactions.

Computer Vision and Visual Search:

Computer vision technologies enable machines to interpret and analyze visual information, driving innovations such as visual search, product recognition, and augmented reality (AR) experiences.

By leveraging computer vision capabilities, businesses can enhance product discovery, enable virtual try-on experiences, and personalize recommendations based on visual cues, enriching the e-commerce journey for users on Shopify platforms.

Predictive Analytics and Machine Learning:

Predictive analytics and machine learning algorithms analyze historical data patterns, identify trends, and generate actionable insights to optimize decision-making and drive personalized experiences.

By harnessing the power of predictive analytics and machine learning, businesses can anticipate customer preferences, forecast demand, and optimize pricing, promotions, and inventory management strategies on Shopify platforms.

Edge Computing and Real-Time Processing:

Edge computing brings computing resources closer to the point of data generation, enabling real-time processing, low-latency interactions, and enhanced user experiences in e-commerce applications.

By leveraging edge computing technologies, businesses can deliver personalized content, streamline checkout processes, and optimize performance for users accessing Shopify platforms from diverse devices and locations.

Blockchain and Decentralized Marketplaces:

Blockchain technology enables secure, transparent, and decentralized transactions, facilitating trustless exchanges, smart contracts, and immutable record-keeping in e-commerce environments.

By embracing blockchain technology, businesses can build trust with users, eliminate intermediaries, and create decentralized marketplaces that empower buyers and sellers to transact securely and transparently on Shopify platforms.

Internet of Things (IoT) and Omnichannel Experiences:

The Internet of Things (IoT) connects physical devices and objects to the internet, enabling seamless integration and data exchange across omnichannel touchpoints.

By leveraging IoT technologies, businesses can create personalized, context-aware experiences, track inventory in real-time, and deliver frictionless shopping experiences that span online and offline channels on Shopify platforms.

By embracing these emerging technologies and integrating AI-driven innovations into Shopify design, businesses can unlock new possibilities for growth, differentiation, and e-commerce excellence. By staying abreast of technological trends, industry developments, and consumer preferences, businesses can position themselves as leaders in the ever-evolving landscape of online retail, empowering e-commerce for the future.

Predictions for the Future of AI in Shopify Design

As AI continues to evolve and shape the landscape of e-commerce, the future of AI in Shopify design holds immense potential for transformative innovation, enhanced user experiences, and sustained growth. Drawing upon current trends and emerging technologies, here are some predictions for the future of AI in Shopify design in the context of "Empowering E-Commerce: Harnessing AI for Shopify Design":

Hyper-Personalization at Scale:

Prediction: AI will enable hyper-personalization at scale, allowing businesses to deliver tailored experiences and recommendations to individual users based on their preferences, behaviors, and context.

Future AI-powered features may include dynamic product recommendations, personalized marketing campaigns, and adaptive user interfaces that adapt in real-time to user interactions and feedback.

Conversational Commerce and Voice-Enabled Experiences:

Prediction: Conversational commerce will become increasingly prevalent, driven by advancements in natural language processing (NLP) and voice recognition technologies.

Future AI-driven capabilities may include voice-enabled shopping assistants, chatbots, and voice-controlled interfaces that enable seamless interactions and transactions on Shopify platforms.

AI-Powered Visual Search and Augmented Reality (AR) Experiences:

Prediction: Visual search and AR experiences will redefine product discovery and exploration in e-commerce, enabling users to search, visualize, and interact with products in immersive ways.

Future AI-driven innovations may include visual search engines, AR-powered virtual try-on experiences, and product visualization tools that empower users to make informed purchase decisions on Shopify platforms.

Predictive Analytics and Inventory Optimization:

Prediction: AI-driven predictive analytics will revolutionize inventory management and supply chain optimization, enabling businesses to forecast demand, optimize stock levels, and prevent stockouts.

Future AI-powered solutions may include predictive inventory algorithms, demand forecasting models, and dynamic pricing strategies that enhance operational efficiency and maximize profitability on Shopify platforms.

Ethical AI Governance and Transparency:

Prediction: Ethical AI governance and transparency will emerge as key priorities for businesses, regulators, and consumers alike, shaping the responsible use of AI technologies in e-commerce.

Future initiatives may include ethical AI frameworks, auditability standards, and transparency measures that promote fairness, accountability, and trustworthiness in AI-driven decision-making on Shopify platforms.

AI-Driven Automation and Workflow Optimization:

Prediction: AI-driven automation will streamline workflows, automate repetitive tasks, and enhance operational efficiency for businesses operating on Shopify platforms.

Future AI-powered solutions may include intelligent chatbots, workflow automation tools, and predictive analytics platforms that empower businesses to focus on strategic initiatives and innovation.

By embracing these predictions and leveraging AI-driven technologies, businesses can unlock new opportunities for growth, differentiation, and e-commerce excellence on Shopify platforms. By staying abreast of technological advancements, industry trends, and consumer expectations, businesses can position themselves as leaders in the ever-evolving landscape of online retail, empowering e-commerce for the future.

Opportunities for Innovation and Growth

In the fast-paced realm of e-commerce, opportunities for innovation and growth abound, fueled by advancements in technology, shifting consumer behaviors, and evolving market dynamics. By harnessing the power of Artificial Intelligence (AI) and embracing innovative approaches to Shopify design, businesses can unlock new avenues for differentiation, engagement, and e-commerce excellence. Here are some key opportunities for innovation and growth in the context of

"Empowering E-Commerce: Harnessing AI for Shopify Design":

Personalized User Experiences:

Opportunity: Personalization remains a cornerstone of e-commerce success, offering businesses the opportunity to deliver tailored experiences and recommendations that resonate with individual users.

Innovation: By leveraging AI-driven algorithms and machine learning models, businesses can analyze user data, predict preferences, and personalize content, products, and promotions to enhance user engagement and drive conversions on Shopify platforms.

Conversational Commerce and AI-Powered Assistants:

Opportunity: Conversational commerce presents an opportunity for businesses to engage with customers in more natural, intuitive ways, fostering meaningful interactions and streamlining the purchasing process.

Innovation: By integrating AI-powered chatbots, virtual assistants, and voice-enabled interfaces into Shopify design, businesses can enable conversational interactions, answer customer inquiries, and guide users through the shopping journey, enhancing convenience and satisfaction.

Visual Search and Augmented Reality (AR) Experiences:

Opportunity: Visual search and AR experiences offer businesses the opportunity to revolutionize product discovery, enabling users to search, visualize, and interact with products in immersive ways.

Innovation: By implementing visual search engines, AR-powered product demonstrations, and virtual try-on experiences on Shopify platforms, businesses can enrich the shopping experience, increase engagement, and reduce friction in the purchase process.

Predictive Analytics and Inventory Optimization:

Opportunity: Predictive analytics empower businesses to forecast demand, optimize inventory levels, and prevent stockouts, enabling more efficient and cost-effective supply chain management.

Innovation: By leveraging AI-driven predictive analytics platforms, businesses can analyze historical data, identify trends, and generate actionable insights to inform inventory decisions, reduce carrying costs, and improve fulfillment processes on Shopify platforms.

Sustainability and Ethical E-Commerce Practices:

Opportunity: Sustainability and ethical considerations are increasingly important to environmentally and socially conscious consumers, creating opportunities for businesses to differentiate themselves and drive brand loyalty.

Innovation: By adopting sustainable sourcing practices, reducing environmental footprints, and promoting transparency in supply chains, businesses can appeal to eco-conscious consumers and foster trust and loyalty on Shopify platforms.

Omnichannel Integration and Seamless Experiences:

Opportunity: Omnichannel integration enables businesses to create cohesive, seamless experiences across online and offline touchpoints, meeting customers wherever they are in their journey.

Innovation: By integrating AI-driven analytics, customer data platforms, and marketing automation tools, businesses can orchestrate personalized, context-aware experiences that span web, mobile, social, and physical channels, driving engagement and loyalty on Shopify platforms.

By embracing these opportunities for innovation and growth and leveraging AI-driven technologies, businesses can unlock new possibilities for differentiation, engagement, and e-commerce excellence on Shopify platforms. By staying agile, customer-centric, and proactive in their approach to innovation, businesses can position themselves as leaders in the ever-evolving landscape of online retail, empowering e-commerce for the future.

CHAPTER 8

CONCLUSION

In the dynamic world of e-commerce, the convergence of Artificial Intelligence (AI) and Shopify design presents boundless opportunities for businesses to innovate, differentiate, and thrive in the digital marketplace. Throughout this journey, we've explored the transformative potential of AI in shaping the future of e-commerce on Shopify platforms, where innovation knows no bounds, and the possibilities are endless.

From personalized user experiences and conversational commerce to visual search and augmented reality, AI-driven innovations are reshaping the way businesses engage with customers, optimize operations, and drive growth. By harnessing the power of AI, businesses can unlock new avenues for differentiation, engagement, and e-commerce excellence, empowering them to stay ahead of the curve and deliver exceptional experiences that resonate with users.

As we reflect on the lessons learned and insights gained, it's clear that the future of e-commerce lies at the intersection of human ingenuity and technological innovation. By embracing AI-driven technologies, businesses can reimagine the shopping experience, foster meaningful connections with customers, and drive sustained growth in the competitive landscape of online retail.

However, with great innovation comes great responsibility. As businesses harness the power of AI, it's imperative to prioritize ethical considerations, data privacy, and transparency to ensure that AI-driven solutions promote fairness, accountability, and trustworthiness in e-commerce environments. By adhering to ethical principles and industry standards, businesses can build trust with users, foster positive relationships, and shape a future where innovation and responsibility go hand in hand.

Recap of Key Points

In "Empowering E-Commerce: Harnessing AI for Shopify Design," we embarked on a journey to explore the transformative potential of Artificial Intelligence (AI) in shaping the future of online retail on Shopify platforms. Throughout our exploration, we uncovered key insights and learned valuable lessons that underscore the power of AI in driving innovation, differentiation, and e-commerce excellence. Here's a recap of the key points discussed in the book:

Introduction to E-Commerce and Shopify:

We began by understanding the foundational concepts of e-commerce and the role of Shopify as a leading e-commerce platform, empowering businesses to create and manage online stores with ease.

Definition and Importance of E-Commerce:

We delved into the definition and significance of e-commerce, highlighting its role in facilitating online transactions, expanding market reach, and driving business growth in the digital age.

Overview of Shopify as an E-Commerce Platform:

We explored the features and capabilities of Shopify as an e-commerce platform, providing businesses with tools and resources to build, customize, and optimize online storefronts for success.

Significance of Design in E-Commerce Success:

We emphasized the importance of design in e-commerce success, highlighting its impact on user experience, brand perception, and conversion rates on Shopify platforms.

Understanding AI in E-Commerce:

We introduced the concept of Artificial Intelligence (AI) and its applications in e-commerce, showcasing how AI-driven technologies can enhance user experiences, optimize operations, and drive growth on Shopify platforms.

Role of AI in E-Commerce:

We explored the pivotal role of AI in e-commerce, including its ability to personalize user experiences, automate tasks, and provide actionable insights to businesses operating on Shopify platforms.

Benefits of Integrating AI into Shopify Design:

We discussed the numerous benefits of integrating AI into Shopify design, such as improved user engagement, enhanced operational efficiency, and increased revenue opportunities for businesses.

Leveraging AI for Shopify Design:

We examined strategies for leveraging AI to enhance Shopify design, including AI-powered product recommendations, personalized user experiences, and automated design optimization techniques.

Ethical and Privacy Concerns in AI-Driven E-Commerce:

We addressed ethical and privacy concerns associated with AI-driven e-commerce, emphasizing the importance of transparency, data security, and regulatory compliance in safeguarding user rights and interests.

133

Future Trends and Innovations in E-Commerce and AI:

We explored emerging trends and innovations in e-commerce and AI, including hyper-personalization, conversational commerce, visual search, and sustainable practices, shaping the future of online retail on Shopify platforms.

In conclusion, "Empowering E-Commerce: Harnessing AI for Shopify Design" serves as a roadmap for businesses seeking to unlock the transformative potential of AI in driving innovation, differentiation, and growth in the competitive landscape of e-commerce. By embracing AI-driven technologies and adopting a customer-centric approach to Shopify design, businesses can position themselves for success and thrive in the ever-evolving digital marketplace.

The Importance of AI in Shaping the Future of E-Commerce

In the book "Empowering E-Commerce: Harnessing AI for Shopify Design," we delve into the critical role that Artificial

Intelligence (AI) plays in shaping the future of online retail. AI stands as a transformative force, revolutionizing the way businesses engage with customers, optimize operations, and drive growth in the digital marketplace. Here, we explore the profound importance of AI in shaping the future of e-commerce:

Personalization and Customer Experience Enhancement:

AI empowers businesses to deliver personalized experiences tailored to individual customer preferences, behaviors, and contexts. Through advanced algorithms and machine learning models, businesses can analyze vast datasets, predict user preferences, and customize product recommendations, advertisements, and promotions on Shopify platforms. This personalized approach enhances user engagement, fosters brand loyalty, and drives conversions, ultimately elevating the overall customer experience in e-commerce.

Automation and Operational Efficiency:

AI-driven automation streamlines and optimizes e-commerce operations, enabling businesses to automate repetitive tasks, streamline workflows, and improve efficiency across the value chain. From inventory management and order processing to customer support and marketing campaigns, AI-powered solutions automate manual processes, reduce human error, and enhance productivity on Shopify platforms. By leveraging AI-driven automation, businesses can focus resources on strategic initiatives, innovation, and value-added activities, driving operational excellence and competitive advantage in the digital landscape.

Predictive Analytics and Business Insights:

AI equips businesses with predictive analytics capabilities, enabling them to anticipate trends, forecast demand, and make data-driven decisions in real-time. By analyzing historical data patterns, identifying correlations, and generating actionable insights, AI-powered analytics platforms empower businesses to optimize pricing strategies, inventory management, and marketing campaigns on Shopify platforms. This data-driven approach enhances agility, responsiveness, and adaptability, enabling businesses to stay ahead of market dynamics and capitalize on emerging opportunities in e-commerce.

Innovation and Differentiation:

AI fuels innovation and differentiation in e-commerce, enabling businesses to pioneer new products, services, and business models that disrupt traditional paradigms and redefine industry standards. By leveraging AI-driven technologies such as natural language processing, computer vision, and machine learning, businesses can explore new frontiers of innovation, such as conversational commerce, visual search, and augmented reality experiences on Shopify platforms. This spirit of innovation drives competitive differentiation, fosters market leadership, and positions businesses for sustained success in the rapidly evolving landscape of online retail.

Adaptability and Future Readiness:

AI enables businesses to adapt and evolve in response to changing market dynamics, consumer preferences, and technological advancements. By embracing AI-driven technologies and cultivating a culture of innovation, businesses can future-proof their operations, anticipate disruptions, and seize opportunities for growth and expansion on Shopify platforms. This adaptability and future readiness ensure that businesses remain agile, resilient, and responsive to the evolving demands of the e-commerce ecosystem, positioning them for long-term success and relevance in a dynamic and competitive marketplace.

In summary, the importance of AI in shaping the future of e-commerce cannot be overstated. From enhancing customer experiences and driving operational efficiency to fueling innovation and future readiness, AI serves as a catalyst for transformation, empowerment, and growth in the digital era. By harnessing the power of AI and embracing a forward-thinking mindset, businesses can unlock new possibilities, navigate complexities, and thrive in the ever-evolving landscape of e-commerce on Shopify platforms.

Final Thoughts on Empowering E-Commerce through AI-driven Shopify Design

In "Empowering E-Commerce: Harnessing AI for Shopify Design," we embarked on a journey to explore the transformative potential of Artificial Intelligence (AI) in revolutionizing the e-commerce landscape on Shopify platforms. As we conclude this exploration, let us reflect on the profound impact of AI-driven Shopify design in empowering businesses to thrive in the digital marketplace.

At its core, e-commerce is not merely about transactions but about meaningful connections, seamless experiences, and lasting impressions. AI serves as a catalyst for innovation, differentiation, and empowerment, reshaping the way businesses engage with customers, optimize operations, and drive growth in the digital era.

Through AI-driven Shopify design, businesses can unlock new possibilities for personalization, automation, and predictive analytics, enhancing the customer journey and driving sustainable value creation. From personalized product recommendations and conversational commerce to visual search and augmented reality experiences, AI enables businesses to redefine user experiences, foster brand loyalty, and unlock new revenue streams in the competitive landscape of online retail.

Moreover, AI-driven Shopify design empowers businesses to navigate complexities, anticipate trends, and stay ahead of the curve in a rapidly evolving marketplace. By embracing AI technologies and cultivating a culture of innovation, businesses can adapt to changing consumer preferences, capitalize on emerging opportunities, and future-proof their operations for long-term success.

However, with great power comes great responsibility. As businesses harness the power of AI, it is imperative to prioritize ethical considerations, data privacy, and transparency to ensure that AI-driven solutions promote fairness, accountability, and trustworthiness in e-commerce environments. By adhering to ethical principles and industry standards, businesses can build trust with users, foster positive relationships, and shape a future where innovation and responsibility go hand in hand.

As we conclude our exploration of empowering e-commerce through AI-driven Shopify design, let us embrace the opportunities that lie ahead, embrace the challenges with resilience and determination, and continue to push the boundaries of what's possible in e-commerce. Together, we can harness the power of AI to create a future where every interaction is meaningful, every experience is exceptional, and every opportunity is within reach.

OTHER BOOKS BY THE AUTHOR

https://www.amazon.com/author/henryeparkins

www.ingramcontent.com/pod-product-compliance
Lightning Source LLC
Chambersburg PA
CBHW060102260726
48658CB00004B/1366